Tyrannosaurus rex

By Julie Haydon

Illustrations by Dave Gunson

T0342763

Contents

Tyrannosaurus rex

Dinosaurs were a group of reptiles that died out millions of years ago.

One of the largest and strongest dinosaurs was the Tyrannosaurus rex.

The Tyrannosaurus rex lived in North America more than 65 million years ago.

This Tyrannosaurus rex skeleton was found in North America in 1990.

This map of North America shows where the skeleton was found.

The Tyrannosaurus rex was about 12 metres long
and weighed about as much
as an African elephant does today.
It walked on its two back legs
and had two small arms and a long tail.

The Tyrannosaurus rex had a thick neck and a big head with powerful jaws and 58 sharp teeth.
Some of its teeth were 30.5 centimetres long – about the length of a school ruler.
The Tyrannosaurus rex grew new teeth to replace teeth that broke or fell out.

teeth of a Tyrannosaurus rex fossil

The Tyrannosaurus rex ate other dinosaurs.

Some scientists think the Tyrannosaurus rex
found and ate dead dinosaurs.
It had a good sense of smell
and this helped it find dead dinosaurs.

The Tyrannosaurus rex may have hunted live dinosaurs. It probably followed large herds of plant-eating dinosaurs, hoping to catch one that was very young, sick or old.

The Tyrannosaurus rex was one of the fiercest and most powerful dinosaurs of its time.

Stuck in the Mud

One day, a Tyrannosaurus rex
walked through the forest
hoping to find a smaller dinosaur to eat.

Suddenly, the Tyrannosaurus rex stopped
and lifted her head.
She could smell a dinosaur nearby.
Then, she heard the call
of a dinosaur in trouble.
A hurt or trapped dinosaur
would make an easy meal.

The Tyrannosaurus rex walked towards the smell
and sound.

As she came out of the forest,
she saw a dinosaur stuck in the mud
in the middle of a murky pool.

The Tyrannosaurus rex walked into the pool,
but with every step she took,
she felt her legs sink into the dark mud.
As the mud got thicker and deeper,
it became harder to pull her legs free,
so the Tyrannosaurus rex stopped.

The other dinosaur was still out of reach,
and it was sinking quickly.
Although the Tyrannosaurus rex was hungry,
she knew it was too dangerous to go any further.

She turned and waded slowly out of the pool.

As the Tyrannosaurus rex stepped onto the bank,
the other dinosaur sank under the mud.

The Tyrannosaurus rex could no longer reach
the dinosaur, so she was no longer interested in it.

She walked back to the forest,
looking for another dinosaur to eat.